Bible Lessons

Volume 1

In The Beginning

by

Gary L. TenBroeke

ISBN 1 897397 17 8

1999

Reprinted 2003

Gospel Standard Trust Publications
12 (b) Roundwood Lane, Harpenden,
Herts, AL5 3DD, England

Contents

Chapter		Page
1.	About God	5
2.	Creation	9
3.	The First Man	13
4.	The First Woman	17
5.	The Fall of Man	21
6.	Sin Found Out	25
7.	Sin Punished	29
8.	The First Children	33
9.	Early Men	37
10.	Noah	41
11.	The Ark	45
12.	The Flood	49
13.	God Remembers Noah	53
14.	God's Covenant with Noah	57
15.	The Tower of Babel	61
	Answers	64

The publishers acknowledge with gratitude the help that Daniel Kaat gave with the illustrations.

Preface

As Timothy knew the holy Scriptures "from a child", so it should be the desire of every Christian parent that, from an early age, their children should be well acquainted with the sacred pages.

The aim of this series is to put before little children, in simple form, the fundamental truths of the faith, by consecutively studying the Bible.

The content being interspersed with questions, colouring texts and illustrations, it is hoped that the interest of younger children will be encouraged.

It is however the desire of the publishers that the Spirit of truth will Himself apply the truth to the hearts of the young children who may read these pages, and teach the way of salvation as only He can.

September 1999

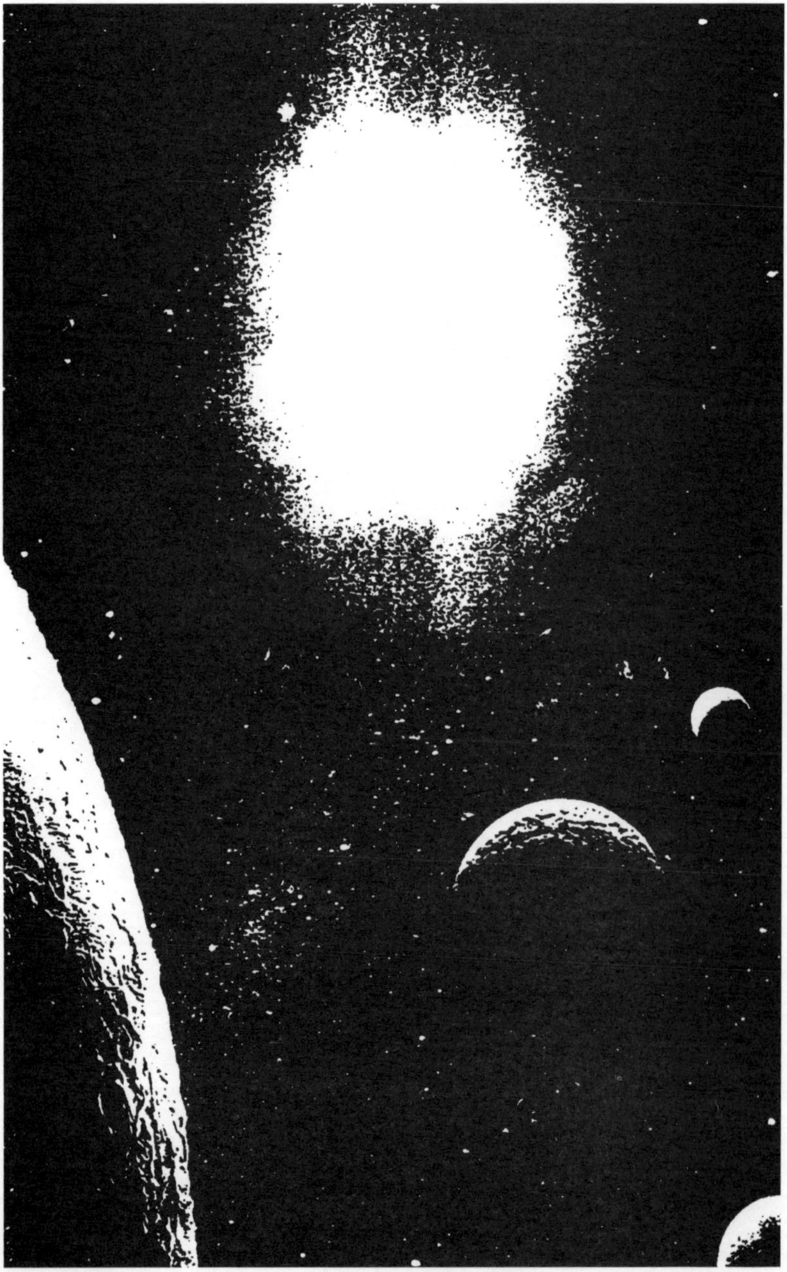

Chapter 1

ABOUT GOD

While thinking about where to begin, my thoughts were directed to God who is the beginning of all things. The Bible tells us that "He is before all things, and by Him all things consist."

God has no beginning and He will never have an end. He always was and He always will be. He is the first and the last. Only God can be both first and last. Adam was the first person made, but he will not be the last person. The last person to be born can never be before Adam. God was before Adam and He will be after the last person.

Perhaps you have wondered if there are more Gods than one. The Bible tells us that there is only one living and true God. God asks the question, "Is there a God beside Me? yea, there is no God; I know not any." A little boy gave a very good answer when asked how he knew there was only one God. He replied, "There is only room for one for He fills heaven and earth."

The Bible tells us all we need to know about God. The Bible tells us that God is in heaven, but He is also everywhere. "The eyes of the Lord are in every place, beholding the evil and the good." The Bible tells us that God is almighty, that He can do everything. [We hope to see a little of this in the next chapter when we look at creation.] We must remember that God cannot lie, because He is the truth. Also, He cannot die, because He is the life.

God is holy; thus He must hate sin. God is light and in Him is no darkness. God is love. God is merciful.

God knows everything. He knows the words we say and the thoughts we think. Nothing can be hidden from Him. God is good. Everything He does is good; it is right; it is perfect.

Questions:

1. What is God before? (two words).
2. Does God have a beginning?
3. How many Gods are there?
4. What tells us all we need to know about God?
5. Where are the eyes of the Lord?

"For Thou art great, and doest wondrous things: Thou art God alone" (Psalm 86. 10).

None is like God, who reigns above,
    So great, so pure, so high;
None is like God, whose name is love,
    And who is always high.

In all the earth there is no spot
    Excluded from His care;
We cannot go where God is not,
    For He is everywhere.

He sees us when we are alone,
    Though no one else can see;
And all our thoughts to Him are known
    Wherever we may be.

And He is before all things, and by Him all things consist.
Colossians 1. 17

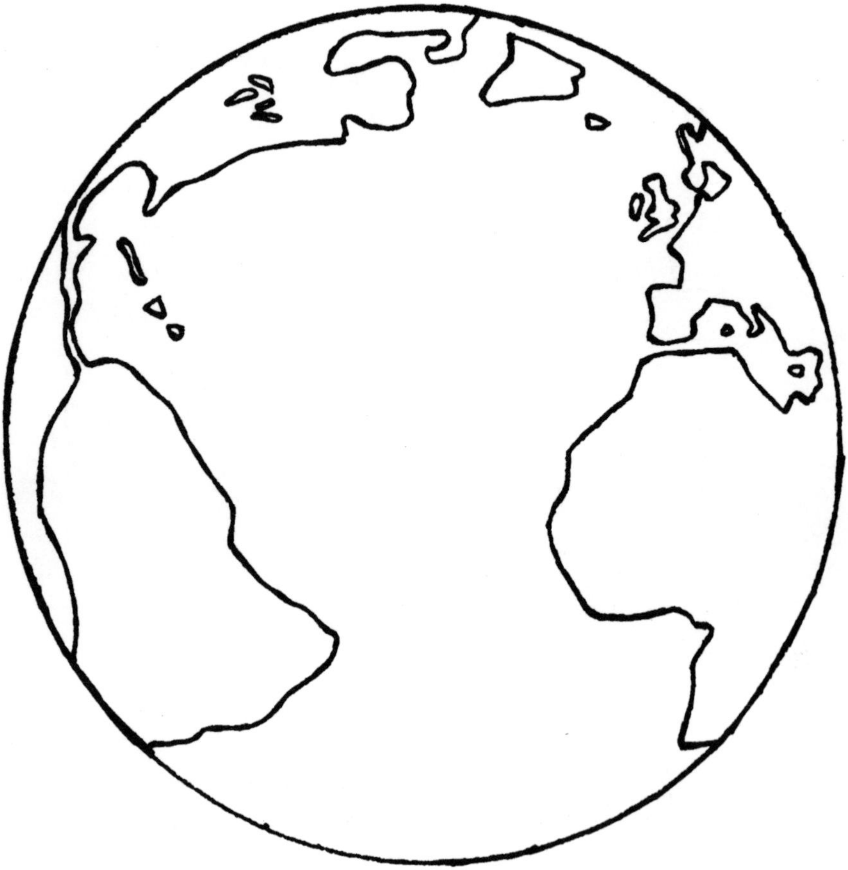

Chapter 2

CREATION

Do you know what the first verse of the Bible is? "In the beginning God created the heaven and the earth." How did God make them? "He spake, and it was done; He commanded, and it stood fast." From what did God make them? He made them out of nothing!

Have you ever made something? If so, you have used other goods or materials to make it. Perhaps you have made a picture by using paper and pencil or paints, or you may have made cookies in which you used flour, eggs, sugar, and butter. Only God can create something out of nothing!

In the last chapter we noticed a few things about God, such as "God is almighty". God asks the question: "Is anything too hard for the Lord?" Creation was an easy thing for God. He needed only to speak. "The voice of the Lord is powerful."

God created the world and all that is in it, in six days.

On the first day God created light and divided it from the darkness. "God called the light Day, and the darkness He called Night."

The second day God created the clouds and the air we breathe.

The third day God created the dry land that is called Earth and everything that grows upon it, and also He made the Seas.

The fourth day God created the sun, the moon, and the stars. They were given for light and for man to measure days, seasons, and years. The Bible tells us: "There is one glory of the sun, and another glory of the moon, and another glory of the stars: for one star differeth from another star in glory."

The fifth day God created all the creatures that live in the sea and all the birds that fly in the air.

The sixth day God made all the animals and creatures that live upon land. Last of all He made man.

The Bible tells us that "God saw everything that He had made, and, behold, it was very good." It was perfect. Nothing had to be made again.

Questions:

6. How did God make the heaven and the earth?
7. From what did God make them?
8. How many days did God take to make everything?
9. What did God make to measure days, seasons, and years?
10. What was the last thing God made?

"For by Him were all things created, that are in heaven, and that are in earth, visible and invisible,...all things were created by Him, and for Him" (Colossians 1. 16).

> Who made the sun so warm and bright
>   To shine through all the day?
> Who makes it sink to rest at night,
>   And rise up in the day?
>
> Who made the shining stars so bright
>   And placed them in the sky?
> Who keeps them twinkling all the night
>   Above our heads so high?
>
> 'Tis God, the heavenly Father good
>   Who made and cares for all,
> For birds, and bees, and shining stars;
>   He knows if one should fall.

In the beginning God created the heaven and the earth. Genesis 1. 1

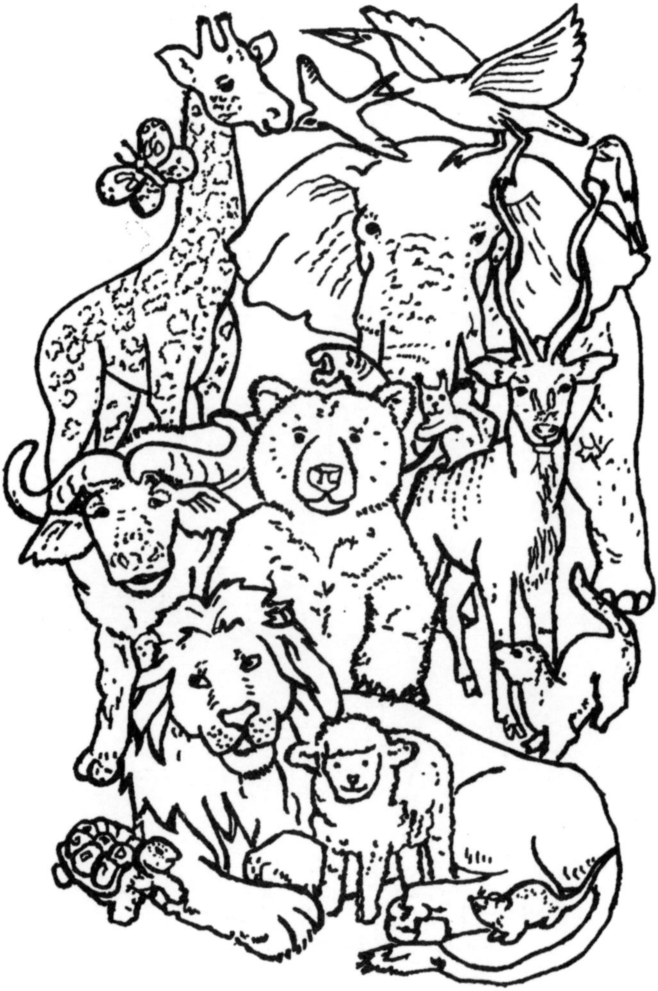

Chapter 3

THE FIRST MAN

When God created the world, He made many great and wonderful things. The mountains and valleys, seas and rivers, sun, moon and stars, animals, fishes and birds, trees and flowers; all of these were very great and wonderful things. Yet the greatest work of creation was the making of man.

Do you know the name God gave the first man? It was Adam.

You were born into the world as a baby. Adam was made a fully grown man.

Man was made different from all the animals. The Bible tells us that he was made "in the image of God". What an honour! He was made perfect, pure (without sin). The Bible tells us, "God hath made man upright."

God formed the body of man from the dust of the ground. He gave him eyes to see with, ears to hear with, a nose to smell with, a mouth to eat with, hands to work with, and feet to walk with. The body, with all these wonderful members, is one part of man.

The second part of man is his soul. How did man receive his soul? The Bible tells us that God "breathed into his (man's) nostrils (nose) the breath of life; and man became a living soul." This living soul was put in man's body. Although you cannot see your soul, just the same it is still there.

God gave man a soul so that he could love God and think upon Him and worship Him. It is the soul that thinks and feels and hopes. It is the soul that also knows right and wrong.

When I was a little boy, our pastor would ask us how long our soul would live. The answer is that it will live as long as God lives, that is for ever. You will remember that God cannot die.

An animal does not have a soul. When it dies, that is the end of the animal. When man dies, his body returns to the dust, but his soul returns to God who gave it.

You can read about this in Genesis chapter 1, verse 26 to chapter 2, verse 7.

Questions:

11. What was the greatest work of God in creation?
12. In whose image was man made?
13. From what did God form man's body?
14. What did God give man so that he could love God?
15. How long will the soul of man live?

"I have made the earth and created man upon it" (Isaiah 45. 12).

> Remember thy Creator,
> While youth's fair spring is bright,
> Before thy cares are greater,
> Before comes age's night.
> While yet the sun shines o'er thee,
> While stars the darkness cheer,
> While life is all before thee,
> Thy great Creator fear.
>
> Remember thy Creator,
> Before the dust returns
> To earth, for 'tis its nature,
> And life's last ember burns.
> Before the God who gave it,
> The spirit shall appear.
> O none but Christ can save it,
> Thy great Creator fear.

I will praise Thee; for I am fearfully and wonderfully made.
Psalm 139. 14

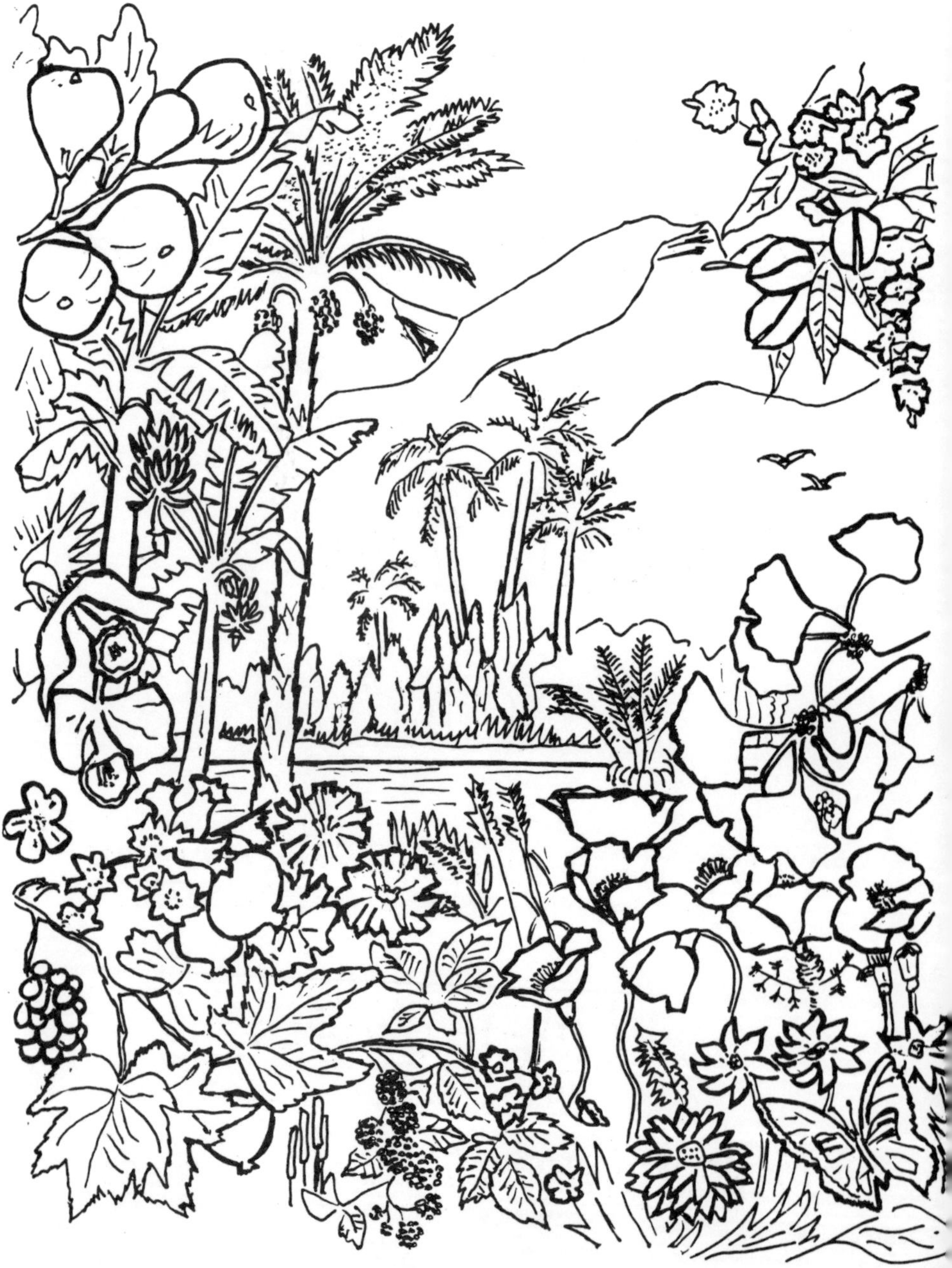

Chapter 4

THE FIRST WOMAN

Do you know where God put man after He had made him? It was in a garden which the Lord God had planted. It was called the Garden of Eden. It was a beautiful garden. It had every tree that was pleasant to the eye and good for food.

Man was put into the garden to care for it. One thing that Adam never had to do in the Garden of Eden was to pull weeds. There were no thorns or thistles either.

Besides keeping the garden, Adam was given another task to do. Have you ever wondered how the animals and birds received their names? "The LORD God ... brought them unto Adam to see what he would call them." What wonderful wisdom God gave to Adam, that he could give a suitable name to each of them! He gave the name of "lion" to one, "camel" to another, "lamb" to another and so forth, in his own language. Each animal was known by the name that Adam gave it. Adam was not afraid of the animals. They were not wild at this time. Adam was made ruler over them. Yet they could not talk to Adam.

Still Adam was all alone in the world, yet not alone, for God was with him, but there was no other person with whom Adam could talk. The Lord God said that it was not good that the man should be alone. He said, "I will make him an help meet (suitable, fitting) for him."

How would God do this? Would He take some more dust to make another person? No. God caused Adam to fall into a deep sleep. While Adam was sleeping, God took one of his ribs and closed up the flesh from where He had taken it. With the rib God made a woman.

When Adam awoke, God brought to him the woman

He had made. How surprised and happy Adam was! How Adam loved her! He would no longer be alone. From now on they would live together and talk together.

Adam called his wife's name "Woman, because she was taken out of Man." Later he would call her Eve.

Together, they could tend the garden and eat the delicious fruits. They were never sick or in pain. They never had any sorrow. They were never upset or angry. Everything was perfect in this lovely garden.

You can read about this in Genesis chapter 2, verses 8 to 25.

Questions:

16. Where did God put the man He made?
17. Who gave the animals and birds their names?
18. What did God say was not good for the man?
19. What did God take from Adam while he was sleeping?
20. What did He make with it?

"And Adam called his wife's name Eve; because she was the mother of all living" (Genesis 3. 20).

> I sing the goodness of the Lord,
>   That filled the earth with food;
> He formed the creatures with His word,
>   And then pronounced them good.
>
> His hand is our perpetual guard,
>   He sees us with His eye;
> And yet how we forget the Lord
>   Who is for ever nigh.

And the Lord God said, It is not good that...man should be alone.
Genesis 2. 18

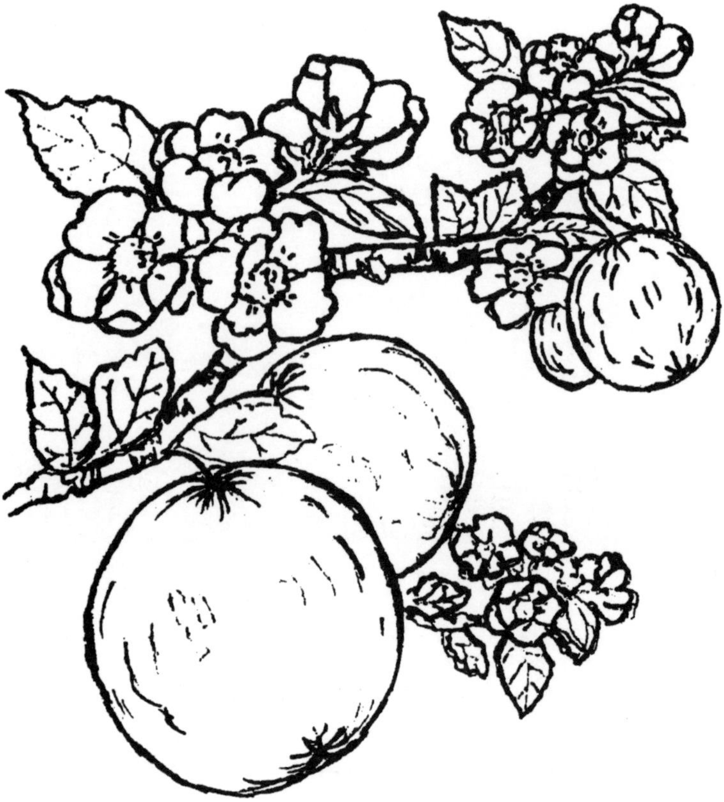

Chapter 5

THE FALL OF MAN

The Garden of Eden was the first home for Adam and Eve. We are sure that no park or garden which man has made could ever be as beautiful as the Garden of Eden.

Adam and Eve were very happy in the garden. They enjoyed sweet union with their Maker. At times the voice of God would talk with them, and they praised Him for all His goodness to them. How they loved and obeyed Him!

God planted a tree in the midst of the garden to prove their love to Him. It was called the "tree of the knowledge of good and evil". The fruit on this tree was beautiful to see. God commanded them not to eat of the fruit of this tree or they would "surely die". However, they might eat freely of every other tree in the garden.

Because their hearts were good, Adam and Eve had no desire to disobey God and eat of the forbidden fruit.

We do not know how long they enjoyed this beautiful, happy time, but we do know a very sad and awful thing happened.

Satan, who is a wicked angel, hates God, and he hated Adam and Eve because they loved and obeyed God. He wished they would be wicked like himself so that they could be his servants. He entered into the garden and hid himself in a serpent.

He came to Eve when she was alone. He asked if God had said, "Ye shall not eat of every tree of the garden." Eve answered, "We may eat of the fruit of the trees of the garden: but of the fruit of the tree which is in the midst of the garden, God hath said, Ye shall not eat of it, neither shall ye touch it, lest ye die."

The serpent told Eve a lie. He said, "Ye shall not surely

die," but "ye shall be as gods, knowing good and evil." We are told that "he is a liar, and the father of it."

Eve believed the serpent instead of believing God. She looked at the tree. She saw the fruit was good for food and pleasant to the eyes. She desired to be wise, and to know evil as well as good. She went to the tree, picked some fruit and ate it. Then she gave some to Adam also and he ate. Adam and Eve disobeyed God. Sin entered the world. This is called the Fall of Man.

A strange something now entered their hearts. It was guilt, fear and shame. They were no longer innocent or sinless.

Questions:

21. Where in the garden did God plant a tree to prove their love to Him?
22. What was this tree called?
23. What did God say would happen if they ate of it?
24. What did Satan hide himself in?
25. When did he come to Eve?

"...By one man sin entered into the world, and death by sin: and so death passed upon all men, for that all have sinned" (Romans 5. 12).

> Man had no sorrow, knew no shame,
>   When first he from his Maker came;
> Good, wise and happy, all was well;
>   But Satan tempted, and he fell.

THE WAGES OF SIN IS DEATH

Romans 6. 23

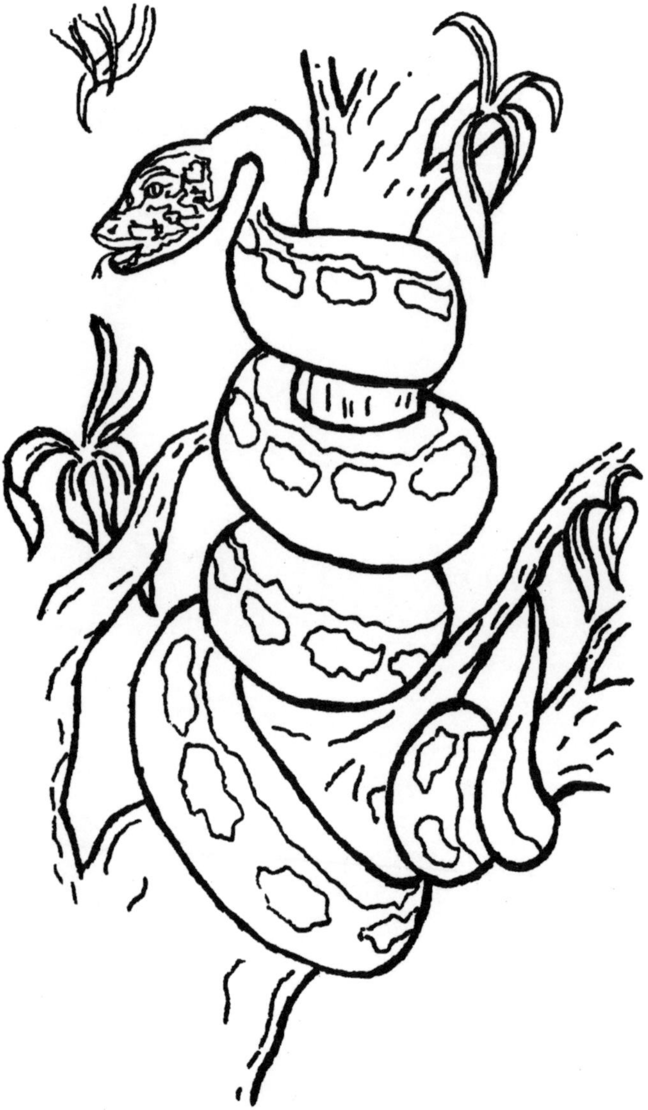

Chapter 6

SIN FOUND OUT

After Adam and Eve disobeyed God, they no longer wanted to be good. They no longer loved God. They did not want God to come and talk with them. Their hearts were now very wicked. They had become servants of Satan.

They now realized that they were naked. Before this, they did not have any shame and did not need any clothing. They quickly sewed fig leaves together to cover themselves.

Soon they "heard the voice of the LORD God walking in the garden". They no longer went to meet God. They were afraid of God. How sad! Worse still, they tried to hide from God.

When you have been naughty does it make you afraid? Perhaps you try to hide, or at least hide the naughty deed. May you ever remember the verse: "Be sure your sin will find you out."

The Lord God called unto Adam, "Where art thou?" Adam answered, "I was afraid, because I was naked; and I hid myself." Then God said, "Who told thee that thou wast naked? Hast thou eaten of the tree, whereof I commanded thee that thou shouldest not eat?"

We must remember that God did not ask these questions because He did not know what they had done. God knows everything! Do you remember the verse we noticed in chapter one: "The eyes of the LORD are in every place, beholding the evil and the good"?

Perhaps, when you have been naughty, you have tried to blame someone or something else. Our hearts are so wicked that we would have someone else to be punished when we are to be blamed. This is just what Adam did. He blamed God for giving him the woman and he blamed the woman for giving him the fruit. It was very wicked of Adam to disobey God, but worse still to blame God.

Eve blamed the serpent for lying to her. She thought she would be happier after eating the fruit; instead, she became very sad. She thought she would be as wise as God; instead, she became wicked like Satan.

God cursed the serpent above all the cattle and beasts of the field. He made the serpent to crawl upon its belly. God put enmity (hatred) between the woman and the serpent.

You can read about this in Genesis chapter 3, verses 7-15.

Questions:

26. To whom did Adam and Eve become servants?
27. What did Adam and Eve use to cover themselves?
28. What did they do when they heard the voice of the Lord God?
29. Whom did Adam blame for his sin?
30. What did God put between the woman and the serpent?

"All things are naked and opened unto the eyes of Him with whom we have to do" (Hebrews 4. 13).

> How happily the moments fled
>   In Eden's garden fair!
> For sin, the source of death and shame
>   Had never entered there.
>
> And man, the lord of that bright place,
>   Could most of all rejoice
> To feel his glorious Maker near,
>   To hear his Maker's voice.

AND BE SURE YOUR SIN WILL FIND YOU OUT.

NUMBERS 32.23

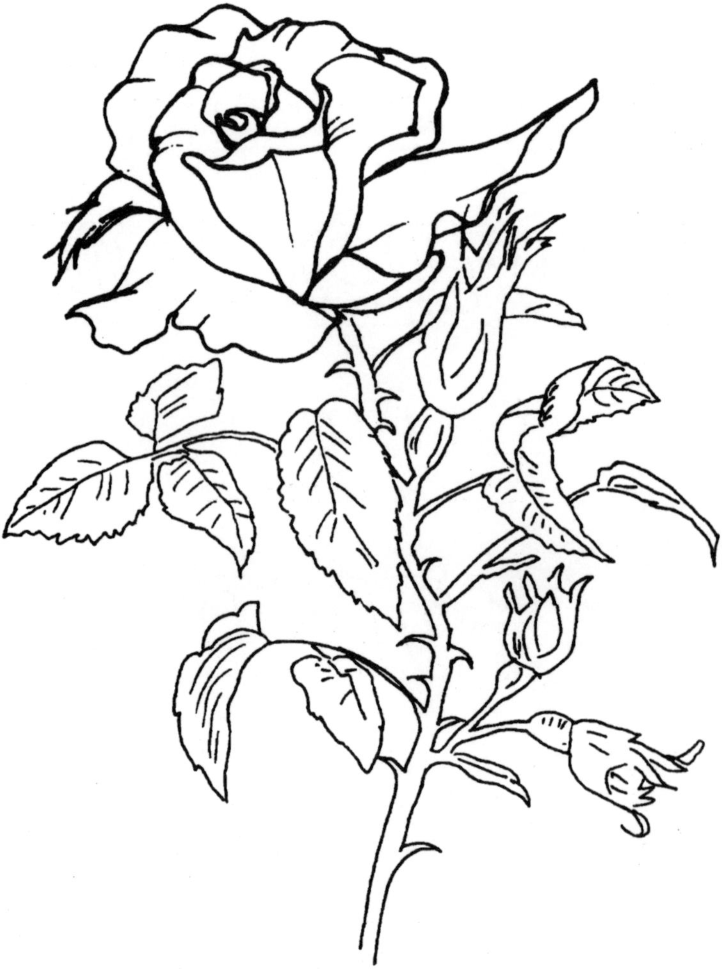

Chapter 7

SIN PUNISHED

When God put enmity (hatred) between the serpent and the woman, He also promised that the seed of the woman would bruise or destroy the serpent (Satan). This was the first promise of a Saviour.

How wonderful that must have sounded to Adam and Eve! They knew that Satan had deceived and destroyed them. The Bible tells us that "The thief (Satan) cometh... to steal, and to kill, and to destroy." Yet God promised that He would destroy the power of Satan.

Still, God would make them know how very wicked they were in disobeying Him. Sin must be punished. God told Eve that she would have much sorrow. Her husband would rule over her. When she should have children, she would also know times of sorrow and pain.

God told Adam that, because he listened to his wife and ate of the tree which God commanded him not to eat of, he too must be punished. Now he would have to work very hard for his food. Perhaps you have watched your father when he was working hard and soon the sweat began to run down his face. God told Adam, "In the sweat of thy face shalt thou eat bread."

He also told Adam that the ground was cursed because of his sin. It would bring forth thorns and thistles which would trouble him.

God told Adam and Eve that their bodies would die and return to dust. Death entered the world because of Adam's sin.

God showed Adam and Eve that He was not satisfied with their covering of fig leaves. Instead He made coats of skins and clothed them. An animal must be killed to provide them clothing.

Besides "the tree of the knowledge of good and evil", there was another wonderful tree in the garden called "the tree of life". Whoever ate of that tree would live for ever.

Now that Adam and Eve had become wicked, God would not allow them to remain in the Garden of Eden lest they should eat of "the tree of life". God sent them out of it for ever.

Through their sin, Adam and Eve lost their beautiful garden home. Perhaps you have lost something and felt very sad and disappointed. Maybe you tried to think back over your ways, to recall where you may have lost it. No doubt Adam and Eve did the same. The Bible tells us to consider our ways.

But could they return to the garden? No. God had put "Cherubims (angels), and a flaming sword which turned every way, to keep the way of the tree of life".

You can read about this in Genesis chapter 3, verses 15-24.

Questions:

31. Whom did God promise to Eve?
32. What would the ground bring forth?
33. What did God say the bodies of Adam and Eve would return to?
34. What did God clothe Adam and Eve with?
35. What kept the way of the tree of life?

> He knew how wicked men had been,
>   And knew that God must punish sin,
> So for His people Jesus said,
>   He'd bear the punishment instead.

Now therefore thus saith the LORD of hosts; Consider your ways. Haggai 1. 5.

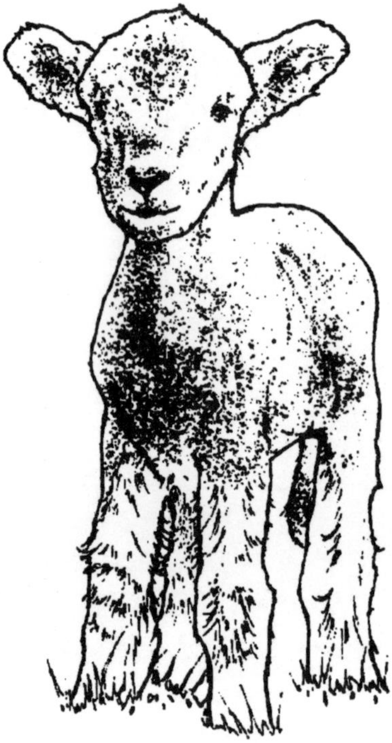

Chapter 8

THE FIRST CHILDREN

How different everything appeared to Adam and Eve after they were put out of the garden! In the garden it was easy and pleasant to tend and gather the fruits. Now Adam had to work long and hard to obtain food for Eve and himself. No doubt there were times when the thorns and thistles pricked and cut his hands while he worked. What a reminder it was to Adam of his sin!

Even though Adam and Eve had become wicked, God still remembered them and one day gave them a precious gift. I expect you like to receive gifts. Well, what gift did God give to Adam and Eve? It was a baby son. Eve called his name Cain, which means, "gotten" or "gained". She said, "I have gotten a man from the LORD." How good that she acknowledged God in it! A little while later, God sent them another son. His name was Abel.

While the two boys were growing up, Adam and Eve had to teach them many things. Likewise, your parents teach you many things. You need to be taught right from wrong, bad from good.

Cain and Abel had to learn which animals were now wild and dangerous. They had to learn how to provide food for themselves. Also, they had to be taught that God required a sacrifice when they worshipped Him. Blood must be shed in order for God to forgive sins.

Soon Cain and Abel grew up and became men. Cain became a tiller of the ground, while Abel kept a flock of sheep. One day Cain brought a gift to the Lord for an offering. It was the fruit which he grew from the ground. Do you remember what God said of the ground? He said it was cursed.

Abel also brought an offering; it was one of his

lambs. We feel sure that it was the best one of his flock. I wonder if you know who was called "the Lamb of God". It was the dear Lord Jesus. The Bible tells us, "By faith Abel offered unto God a more excellent sacrifice than Cain."

God showed Cain and Abel that He had rejected Cain's offering and accepted Abel's. Cain became very angry with God and Abel. God told Cain that, if he had offered as Abel did, his offering would have been accepted too. But Cain did not want to obey God. Because of sin in our hearts, we become angry when we cannot have our way. One day, while he and Abel walked in a field, Cain did a dreadful thing. He killed Abel! The Bible tells us Cain slew Abel, "Because his own works were evil, and his brother's righteous". Abel's blood ran out and soaked into the ground.

God asked Cain, "Where is Abel thy brother?" Cain told a wicked lie. He said, "I know not: Am I my brother's keeper?" God said, "The voice of thy brother's blood crieth unto Me from the ground." Then God punished Cain. No longer would the ground grow very much for him. He must flee into a far country, and go out from the presence of the Lord.

How sad it must have been for Adam and Eve to see their dear son Abel dead! They knew it was their own sin which had brought death and sorrow into the world.

Questions:

36. What were the names of the first children?
37. What did God require when they worshipped Him?
38. What did Abel offer unto God?
39. Who was called the Lamb of God?
40. What did Cain do to Abel?

By faith Abel offered unto God a more excellent sacrifice than Cain. Hebrews 11.4

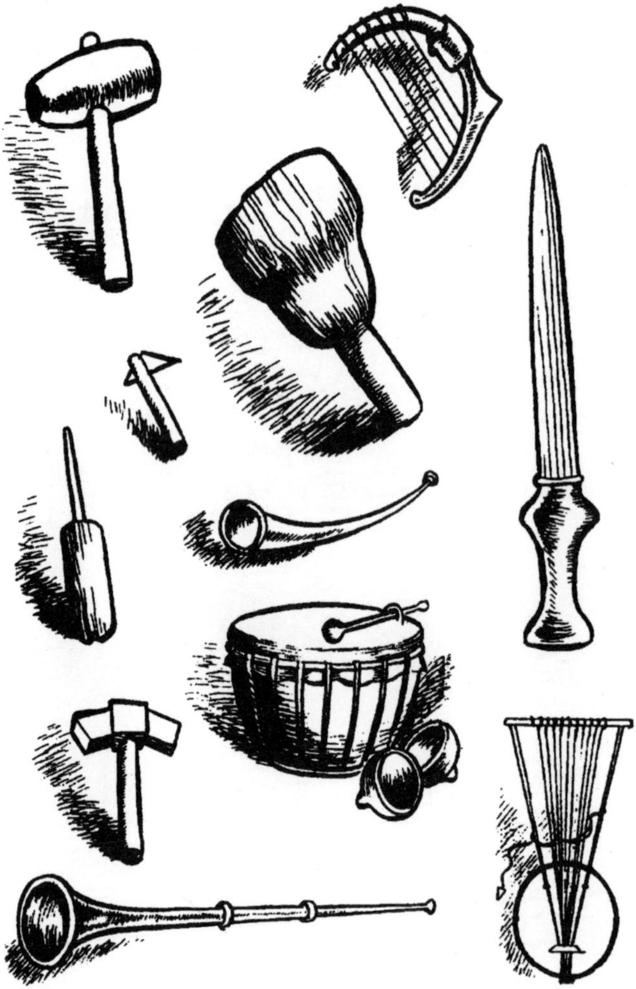

Chapter 9

EARLY MEN

When Cain went out from the presence of the Lord and away from his father and mother, he took his wife with him. Adam and Eve were given daughters as well as sons, one of whom became the wife of Cain.

In time, Cain and his wife had a baby who was named Enoch. Enoch grew up and had children, who likewise grew up and also had children. After a while, a son was born named Lamech, who had three sons. Their names were Jabal, Jubal and Tubal-cain.

Jabal was the first man to make a tent to live in. Jubal was skilful in making musical instruments, such as the harp. Tubal-cain discovered that, by melting brass and iron, he could make tools and weapons.

Some people believe that early men lived very simple or crude lives and were unlearned. However, the Bible tells us that these descendants of Cain were very clever. God gave them great wisdom and skill to find and use the many wonderful things that He put in the earth when He created it.

Cain and his descendants (children, grandchildren, greatgrandchildren, etc.) lived without God. How sad when we think we can do without God! By nature our hearts are just like that.

However, God would not have all the people in the world to live like Cain and his children, without any thought of Him.

God gave Adam and Eve another son in place of Abel, whom Cain killed. Eve called him Seth. What a comfort he was to them now that Abel was dead and Cain had moved far away!

Seth soon grew up and had a son of his own, who was called Enos. God put a difference between Seth and his children, and Cain and his children. The Bible tells us that Seth and his children began "to call upon the name of the Lord".

Adam was one hundred and thirty years old when Seth was born. For Adam this was very young, because he would live to be nine hundred and thirty years old. Many of Adam's children lived a long time also. In this way the world became full of people.

The man who lived the longest was Methuselah. He lived to be nine hundred and sixty-nine years old. How strong their bodies must have been!

While Methuselah lived to be the oldest man, his father did not live nearly so long. His father's name was Enoch, and he lived only three hundred and sixty-five years. However, he did not die. You may be wondering whatever happened to him if he did not die. God did something very wonderful for him. Enoch loved God and prayed to Him. The Bible tells us that "he pleased God", and "walked with God: and he was not; for God took him." God took him straight to heaven.

You can read about this in Genesis chapter 4, verses 16-26, and chapter 5, verses 1-27; also in Hebrews chapter 11, verses 5 and 6.

Questions:

41. What son was given to Adam and Eve in place of Abel?
42. What did Seth and his children begin to do?
43. How long did Methuselah live?
44. With whom did Enoch walk?
45. What happened to Enoch?

Quicken us, and we will call upon Thy name.

Psalm 80. 18

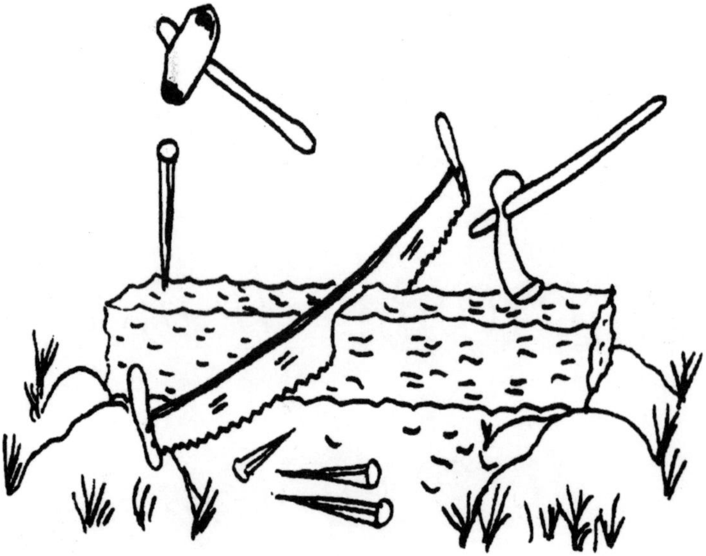

Chapter 10

NOAH

Do you remember what we noticed about Enoch in the last chapter? He was a good man who pleased God and walked with Him. Sadly, most of the people were not like Enoch for they were very wicked. The Bible tells us, "God saw that the wickedness of man was great in the earth. and that every imagination of the thoughts of his heart was only evil continually." "The LORD looked down from heaven upon the children of men, to see if there were any that did understand, and seek God. They are all gone aside, they are all together become filthy: there is none that doeth good, no, not one."

This great multitude had no desire to please God. They did not love Him. They did not thank Him for all the provisions of food and shelter. They did not teach their children to follow after that which was good and to forsake the evil. "They did not like to retain God in their knowledge."

God was sorry that He had made man on the earth. "The LORD said, I will destroy man whom I have created from the face of the earth; both man, and beast, and the creeping thing, and the fowls of the air."

Do you recall the difference that God put between the children of Cain and the children of Seth? They began to "call upon the name of the LORD". That difference was seen in one of Enoch's great-grandchildren. His name was Noah. We are told that "Noah was a just man and perfect in his generations, and Noah walked with God."

Perhaps you are wondering how Noah could walk with God, when the people all around him were living so wickedly. The Bible gives us the answer. "But Noah found grace in the eyes of the LORD." Without grace Noah would have been no different from the rest of the people. God only can give such grace. The Bible tells us He is "the God of all grace". Grace is a very great word. It is a favour that God shows to undeserving sinners.

The earth was filled with violence through the wickedness of the people. Therefore God told Noah that He would destroy the earth and all flesh by a flood of waters, on account of their sins.

Just as God did something wonderful for Enoch in taking him to heaven, so He would preserve Noah in the great flood of His judgment. He commanded Noah to build an ark (a great ship), so that he and his wife and his sons with their wives might be saved.

You can read about this in Genesis chapter 6, verses 5 to 17 and Psalm 14, verses 2 and 3.

Questions:

46. How many did God find that would seek Him?
47. What did Noah find in the eyes of the Lord?
48. To whom does God give His grace? (two words)
49. How would God destroy the earth?
50. What was Noah told to build?

"Noah was a just man and perfect in his generations, and Noah walked with God" (Genesis 6. 9).

> Like as the days of Noah were
>   So shall they also be,
> When Christ, the Son of man, shall come,
>   Whom every eye shall see.

But Noah found grace in the eyes of the Lord.

Genesis 6. 8

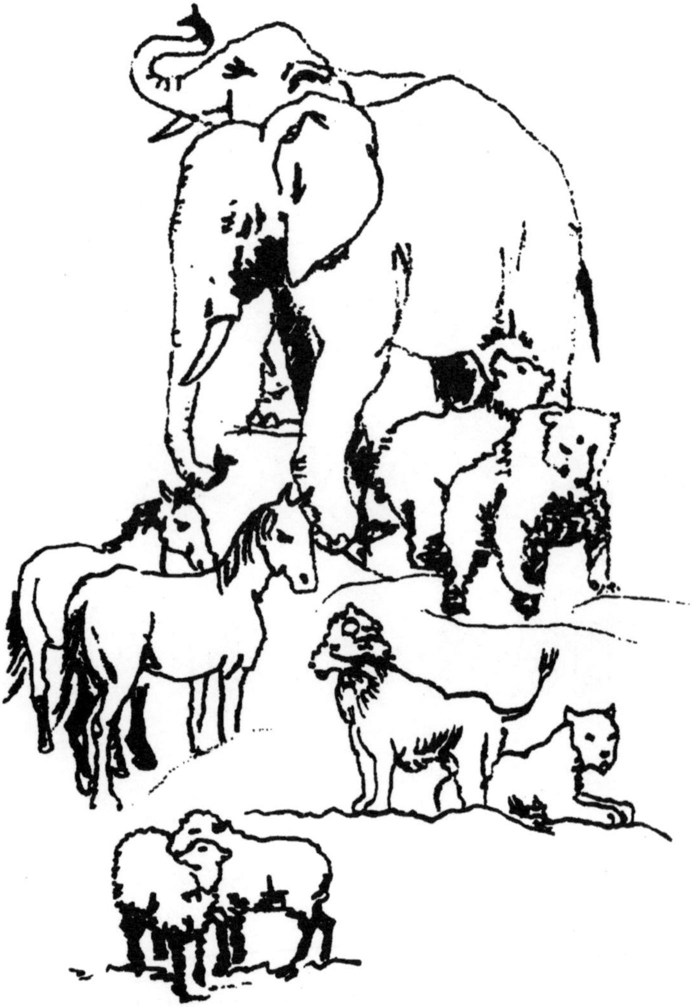

Chapter 11

THE ARK

By Noah's time there were very many people living upon the earth. Their hearts were full of sin. Thus their thoughts and words and deeds were all very wicked. God said that He would "destroy them with the earth".

Noah was given three sons, whose names were Shem, Ham and Japheth.

Then God told Noah that He was going to destroy the world with a flood. Noah believed God. "By faith Noah, being warned of God of things not seen as yet, moved with fear, prepared an ark to the saving of his house."

God told Noah how to build the ark. He told him just how big to make it and what materials to use.

First, he was told to make it from gopher wood. A very strong wood would be needed to protect them from the great waters of the flood. It must have been very hard work to cut down the trees and saw them into boards to build the ark. Perhaps, when Noah's sons grew up, they helped him in the work.

He also had to cover the inside and outside of the ark with pitch, so that the water could not come through the cracks.

He had to make it very large, so that there would be room for at least two of every kind of animal and fowl that breathed. It was to be nearly five hundred feet long, eighty feet wide, and fifty feet high. It was to have three storeys inside: a lower, second, and third level, with rooms in them.

There was to be a window to the ark, which would perhaps give some light and fresh air. There was also to be a door in the side of the ark, so they and the animals could enter.

God told Noah to gather food into the ark for the animals and himself. A great deal of food would be needed, for the flood was to last a long time.

Noah began to build, "according to all that God commanded him". It took him a very long time to build, perhaps over a hundred years.

While Noah was building the ark, he also preached to the people. He warned them that God was going to send a flood and punish them for their wickedness. The people did not believe Noah.

No doubt many of them thought Noah was a foolish man and mocked him. They did not believe that God would send a flood. They kept doing their wicked things.

You can read about this in Genesis chapter 6, verses 10-22, Hebrews chapter 11, verse 7, 1 Peter chapter 3, verse 20 and 2 Peter chapter 2, verse 5.

Questions:

51. What were the names of Noah's sons?
52. What was the ark to be made from?
53. Where was Noah told to put the pitch?
54. Where was the door placed in the ark?
55. What else did Noah do while he built the ark?

> When Noah, with his favoured few,
>   Was ordered to embark,
> Eight human souls, a little crew,
>   Entered on board his ark.
>
> In Christ, his Ark, he safely rides,
>   Not wrecked by death or sin.
> How is it he so safe abides?
>   The Lord has shut him in.

By faith Noah, moved with fear, prepared an ark.
Hebrews 11. 7

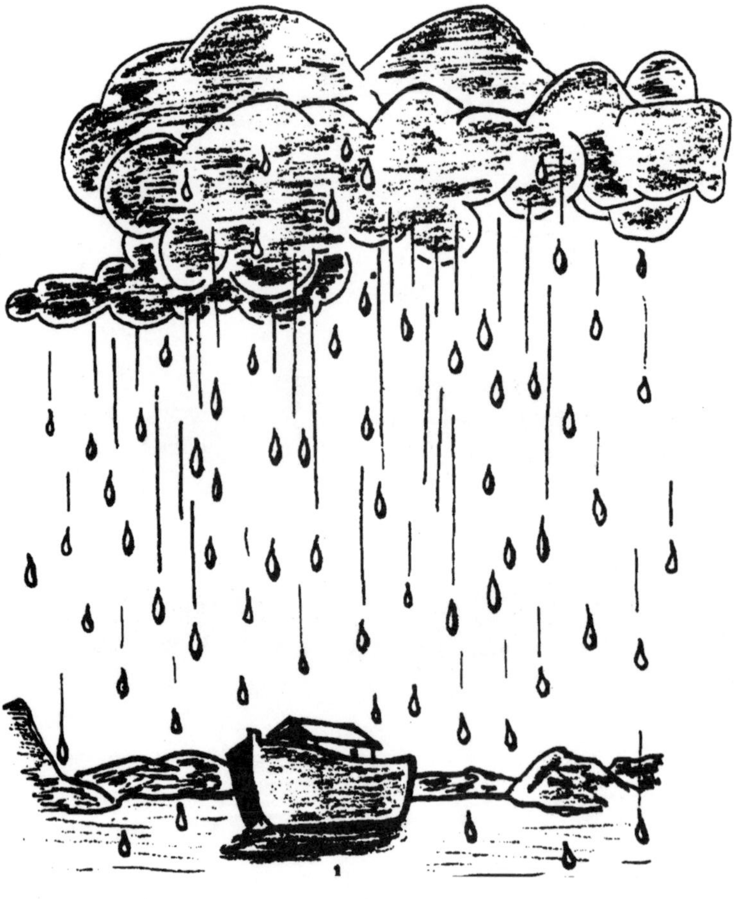

Chapter 12

THE FLOOD

One day the ark was completed and Noah stored all kinds of food in it. Everything was now ready. To many people it must have been a very strange sight to see a big ship so far from water.

God then said to Noah, "Come thou and all thy house into the ark." What a gracious word this is! Noah was not commanded to go into the ark, but rather he was invited to *come*. We may understand by this that God would be with him in the ark.

Noah went into the ark with his wife. His three sons Shem, Ham and Japheth also went in with their wives.

Then the animals started to enter the ark. They came by twos, a male and a female of unclean beasts and by sevens, a male and a female of every clean beast. The fowls of the air came by sevens also.

How amazed the people round the ark must have been! What a strange sight, to see lions, bears, sheep, and deer, and all other animals marching into the ark! Even upon seeing the animals act so strangely, the people still did not believe that God would send a flood.

When all the animals, birds, and creeping things were safe inside the ark, the Lord shut the door. No one could go out and no one could get in.

Finally, the day that God had promised arrived. It started to rain. Never was there rain like it. The Bible says, "The same day were all the fountains of the great deep broken up, and the windows of heaven were opened." The rain poured upon the earth for forty days and forty nights.

Ever so quickly, the water covered the land and entered the homes of the people. Now they believed that Noah had told the truth, but it was too late. What despair filled their hearts! Where could they go? Soon the waters were over the roofs of their homes. Perhaps some tried to flee to the hills and mountains. Frightened animals also hurried to seek a place of refuge. The great flood of waters swept them all away. All the high hills and the mountains were covered. The water ascended fifteen cubits (about twenty feet) above the highest mountain.

The water lifted up the ark from the earth and it floated safely upon the waters. Outside the ark was death and destruction. Inside the ark there was peace and safety. The ark is a beautiful type (picture) of the Lord Jesus Christ. He is the place of safety to all who flee unto Him for refuge from the wrath of God against sin.

"And every living substance was destroyed which was upon the face of the ground, both man, and cattle, and the creeping things, and the fowl of the heaven; and they were destroyed from the earth: and Noah only remained alive, and they that were with him in the ark."

You can read about this in Genesis chapter 7.

Questions:

56. What word did God say to Noah when He invited him into the ark?
57. Who shut the door?
58. How many days and nights did it rain?
59. What was outside the ark?
60. Who is the ark a type of?

> The ark, the ark, and it alone,
>   Was safety in the flood,
> So Jesus, and no other name,
>   Saves sinners by His blood.

His children shall have a place of refuge.

Proverbs 14. 26

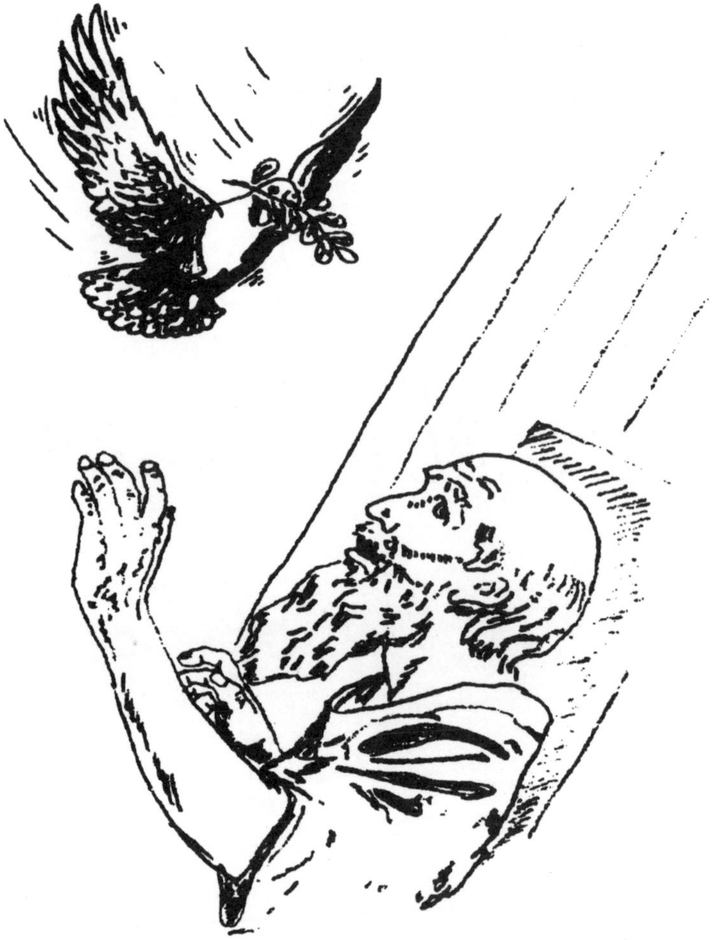

Chapter 13

GOD REMEMBERS NOAH; NOAH WAITS UPON GOD

What a long time it must have seemed to Noah and his family while they were in the ark! Yet the Bible tells us, "God remembered Noah, and every living thing... that was with him in the ark." We wonder if it was Noah's prayerful desire every day, that God would remember him for good.

At God's command, "The fountains also of the deep and the windows of heaven were stopped, and the rain from heaven was restrained."

But where was all the water to go? How could it be dried up, that the earth might be seen again? God always knows what He will do. He caused a wind to blow over the earth. Slowly the waters began to go down. What wonderful things God is able to do with His wind! He divided the waters of the sea with His wind. Also, "He commandeth, and raiseth the stormy wind, which lifteth up the waves thereof." "He bringeth the wind out of His treasuries."

At the end of five months the ark came to a standstill. It had finally come to rest upon the mountains called Ararat.

The water continued dropping down the mountain side. After another two and a half months the tops of the mountains could be seen.

Noah waited forty days longer. Then he opened the window of the ark and sent forth a raven. A raven is a very strong bird. It never returned to the ark but flew "to and fro, until the waters were dried up from off the earth".

Then Noah sent forth a dove to see if the waters were dried up from the earth. The dove was not as strong as the raven. She could not keep flying without any rest. Because the waters were still covering the earth the little dove could find no rest. So she returned to the ark, and Noah "put forth his hand, and took her, and pulled her in unto him into the ark."

Noah waited seven days and sent forth the dove again. This time the dove stayed out longer, and in the evening returned to the ark with an olive leaf in her mouth. Now Noah knew that the waters were drying up from off the earth.

After waiting another week, Noah sent forth the dove again. This time she did not return to him.

After waiting another month, Noah began to remove the covering of the ark and looked upon the earth. What a lovely sight it must have been!

Still Noah waited in the ark another two months. What patience he needed! A year and ten days had passed since they entered the ark. They waited for God's command to go forth from the ark with every living thing.

You can read about this in Genesis chapter 8, verses 1-17.

Questions:

61. God _____ Noah. (Fill in the word).
62. What did God use to dry up the waters of the flood?
63. What did the dove bring back in her mouth the second time?
64. How long had Noah and his family been in the ark?
65. What did they wait for to go forth from the ark?

Remember me, O L ORD , with the favour that Thou bearest unto Thy people.
Psalm 106. 4

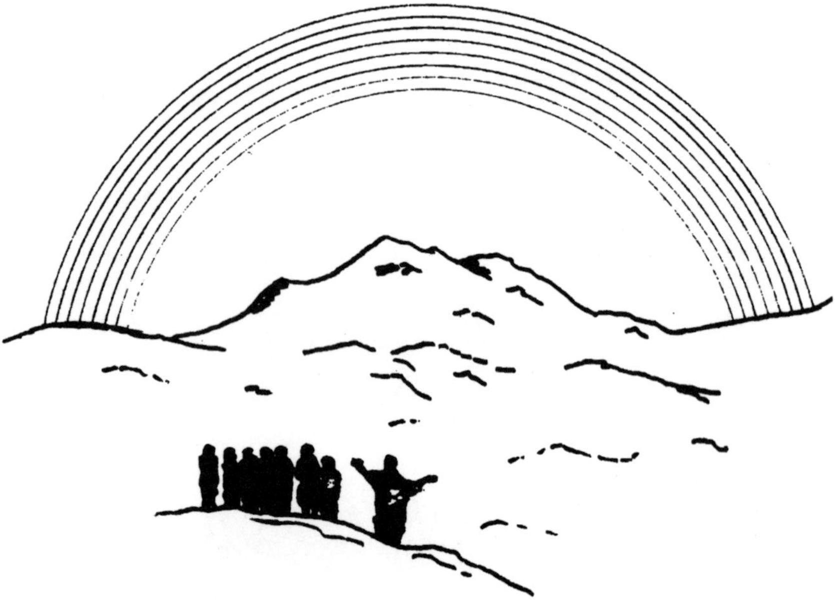

Chapter 14

GOD'S COVENANT WITH NOAH

At the appointed time God told Noah, "Go forth of the ark, thou, and thy wife, and thy sons, and thy sons' wives with thee." What a strange feeling it must have been! Before they entered the ark the world was full of people; now they were the only ones left.

Also he was to bring forth the animals. Out flew the birds so happy in their flight! The animals began to separate into the forests or fields, each looking for a place most suitable for them to live and have their young.

What do you think was the first thing that Noah and his family did when they came from the ark? Did they start to build a home? Or did they try to find some food to eat? No, the first thing they did was to offer thanks and praise to God for preserving them when all others were destroyed.

"And Noah builded an altar unto the Lord; and took of every clean beast, and of every clean fowl, and offered burnt offerings on the altar." The Lord was pleased with the offerings and accepted them. "And the Lord smelled a sweet savour; and the Lord said in His heart, I will not again curse the ground any more for man's sake;...While the earth remaineth, seedtime and harvest, and cold and heat, and summer and winter, and day and night shall not cease."

God then blessed Noah and his sons and told them to have many children so that the earth might be filled with people again.

God gave a commandment to them that they must not kill one another as Cain slew Abel. If any should kill another, he must be put to death. God explained why He gave this law regarding the life of man. "For in the image of God made He man."

God then did something very wonderful for Noah, his sons and for all mankind and for every living thing. He made a covenant with them. A covenant is a most earnest oath or promise.

God's covenant (promise) was that He would never again cut off all flesh or destroy the earth with a flood. God told Noah that He would give him a sign or token of this promise by putting a bow in a cloud. No doubt you have seen God's sign many times. It is a beautiful rainbow. Perhaps you have noticed that the darker the cloud is the brighter the rainbow appears in it. Thus God's dear people often find that the darker and heavier their trials are, the brighter God's promises shine. Whenever you see a rainbow God would have you remember His promise that never again will He destroy the whole world with a flood.

God called it an everlasting covenant. He said, whenever He placed a bow in the cloud, He would look upon it and remember His covenant with every living creature.

You can read about this in Genesis chapter 8, verses 20-22 and chapter 9, verses 1-17.

Questions:

66. What did Noah build?
67. What did Noah offer?
68. What did God make with Noah and every living thing?
69. What sign did God give?
70. Where did God put the bow?

"My covenant will I not break, nor alter the thing that is gone out of my lips" (Psalm 89. 34).

He will ever be mindful of His covenant.

Psalm 111. 5

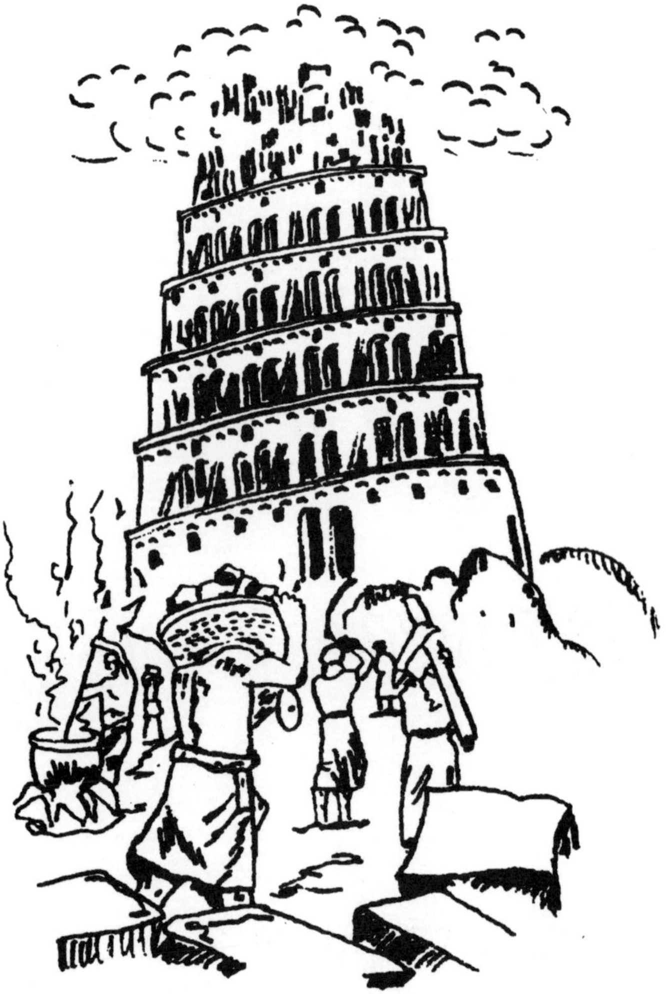

Chapter 15

THE TOWER OF BABEL

It was a new beginning for Noah and his sons and their wives following the flood. The wicked people with their wicked works had been destroyed. No one mocked them any more when they worshipped God.

Noah and his sons began to build homes to live in. Soon God gave Shem, Ham and Japheth children. These children grew up and built homes for themselves. They had children also, and after some years they began to build cities.

As the number of people increased, they moved farther away from the mountains of Ararat. While they journeyed to the south and east, they came to a plain (flat area) in the land of Shinar. The land was well watered with two great rivers, the Tigris and the Euphrates, running on either side of it. Also it was very large, providing plenty of room.

Again men displayed their rebellion against God. He had told Noah and his sons, "Be fruitful, and multiply, and replenish (fill) the earth." God had told them that they were to be scattered through the earth. But they said to each other, "Let us build us a city and a tower, whose top may reach unto heaven; and let us make us a name, lest we be scattered abroad upon the face of the whole earth." So the people prepared themselves to work.

The soil found in Shinar was very suitable for making bricks. A great many people worked very hard and soon they had a large supply of bricks ready for building.

What a busy people! Some were making more bricks, while others were making mortar from slime. Still others were carrying the bricks and mortar to the workmen who were starting to build the tower. It seemed that everything was going very well and everyone expected the tower would soon be finished.

One day a visitor came to see the tower. It was God. He did not talk to the builders, nor was He seen. The people did not even know that He was there. They had forgotten God. By nature we are just like them. God was not pleased with their work. He knew that they would become more sinful if the tower was completed. The only thing they thought about was their name and their city. What could be done to stop the people from building?

Until this time everyone spoke the same language. Now God changed their language. They no longer could understand each other. The members of one family could not understand what their neighbours were saying. The work was stopped. The people who spoke one language joined together and moved away from the city. Others did the same. Now the people were scattered throughout the world and spoke many different languages.

The name of the tower was called Babel, which means "confusion" because God confused the people by changing the language they spoke.

You can read about this in Genesis chapter 11, verses 1-9.

Questions:

71. What did the people begin to build?
72. Who came to see their work?
73. What did He do to stop them?
74. What happened to the people after their language was changed?
75. What was the tower called and what did it mean?

> Come, my dear child, and hear
>   A loving father speak:
> Before you plan, in godly fear
>   Always God's blessing seek.

Except the L̦ord build the house, they labour in vain that build it

Psalm 127. 1

ANSWERS

1. All things.
2. No.
3. One.
4. The Bible.
5. In every place.
6. He spake and it was done.
7. From nothing.
8. Six days.
9. The sun, moon and stars.
10. Man.
11. The making of man.
12. God's.
13. Dust.
14. A soul.
15. For ever.
16. In the Garden of Eden.
17. Adam.
18. To be alone.
19. A rib.
20. Woman.
21. In the midst of the garden.
22. The tree of the knowledge of good and evil.
23. They would surely die.
24. A serpent.
25. When she was alone.
26. Satan.
27. Fig leaves.
28. Tried to hide.
29. God and the woman.
30. Enmity (or hatred).
31. A Saviour.
32. Thorns and thistles.
33. Dust.
34. Coats of skins.
35. Cherubims and a flaming sword.
36. Cain and Abel.
37. A blood sacrifice.

38. A lamb.
39. The Lord Jesus.
40. He killed him.
41. Seth.
42. Call upon the name of the Lord.
43. 969 years.
44. God.
45. God took him.
46. None.
47. Grace.
48. Undeserving sinners.
49. By a flood.
50. An ark.
51. Shem, Ham and Japheth.
52. Gopher wood.
53. Inside and outside.
54. In the side.
55. Preached to the people.
56. Come.
57. God.
58. Forty.
59. Death and destruction.
60. The Lord Jesus Christ.
61. Remembered.
62. Wind.
63. An olive leaf.
64. A year and ten days.
65. God's command.
66. An altar.
67. Burnt offerings.
68. A covenant.
69. A rainbow.
70. In a cloud.
71. A tower.
72. God.
73. Changed their language.
74. They were scattered.
75. Babel. Confusion.

OTHER BOOKS AVAILABLE

Bible Doctrines Simply Explained: by B.A. Ramsbottom
A simple presentation of Christian doctrine.
The Old is Better: by A.J. Levell
The Authorised Version of the Bible defended.
Spirit of Truth: by J.R. Broome
Some aspects of charismatic teaching examined.
Christmas Evans: by B.A. Ramsbottom
Welsh evangelist of 18th century.
Christian Marriage and Divorce: by L.S.B. Hyde
Marriage and divorce in the light of Scripture teaching.
Cremation-Not for Christians: by A.J. Levell
Why a Christian should be buried and not cremated.
Miracles of Jesus (series of 7): by B.A. Ramsbottom
Simply retold and illustrated for young children.
Stranger Than Fiction: by B.A. Ramsbottom
The Life of William Kiffin, 17th century preacher and M.P.
Reformation and Counter Reformation: by J.R. Broome
Attempts to change the Protestant constitution.
John Knox: by J.R. Broome
16th century Scottish reformer.
Servant of a Covenant God: by J.R. Broome
Life and times of John Warburton of Trowbridge.
More Than Notion: by J.H. Alexander
Spiritual experiences of a remarkable group of people.
The Things Most Surely Believed Among Us:
by William Gadsby
A catechism containing the doctrines of divine truth.
Creation: by John Barker
The Bible consistent with true science.
John Gill: by J.R. Broome
18th century theologian and Bible commentator.

In All Their Affliction: by Murdoch Campbell
Words of comfort for Christians.
The Seceders: by J.H. Philpot
The story of J.C. Philpot and William Tiptaft.
Unanswered Prayer: by G.D. Buss
The difficulty of seemingly unanswered prayer.
Sin and Salvation: by J.C. Philpot
The two sides to real religion.
Gadsby's Hymns
A selection of hymns compiled by William Gadsby.
To Glory in a Blaze: by J.R. Broome
The 16th century English martyrs.
Six Remarkable Ministers: by B.A. Ramsbottom
How God made them to be ministers of the gospel.
Divine Guidance: by B.A. Ramsbottom
How may I know God's will?
John Kershaw; an autobiography
Pastor for 50 years in Rochdale.
Why Denominations?: by J.A. Watts
The dangers of modern ecumenism examined.
Bibles
The Word of God. A selection of the Authorised Version.

For a full list of publications please write to:

Gospel Standard Trust Publications
12(b) Roundwood Lane
Harpenden
Herts, AL5 3DD
England.